D0713164

Life With Riv

Fulton Books, Inc.
Meadville, PA

Published by Fulton Books 2021

ISBN 978-1-64654-183-6 (paperback)
ISBN 978-1-64952-773-8 (hardcover)
ISBN 978-1-64654-184-3 (digital)

Printed in the United States of America

Life With Riv

A DOG's GUIDE to the SAN FRANCISCO BAY AREA AND BEYOND

Charlotte Waikart

MY PUPPY LIFE

Hi! I'm a two-month old Bernedoodle puppy here. I don't really know what the world is about yet but I'm ready to learn all about it.

My human best friend Brett, named me Sir Rivington but everyone calls me Riv. We live in San Francisco and travel to many fun places in the Bay Area. We also drive to Southern California, Napa Valley, and Lake Tahoe. Sometimes Brett drives us to various City parks to get our exercise.

When I was a puppy, I stayed in our apartment and splashed in the water on our outside patio. I am an 85 pound Bernedoodle now.

I like playing in the water but my favorite games are chasing sticks and tennis balls that Brett throws for me.

We have fun everyday in San Francisco!

Lafayette Park is high on a hill across the street from some apartments. Brett walks me to the Park every day to play and make friends.

I think this big Bernese Mountain dog recognizes that I am part Bernese too so we sniff to say "hello". We dogs sniff a lot to say "hello" since we can not shake hands.

I made a new friend in the Park today.

Lafayette Park in
Pacific Heights—
the Park is bordered on
Gough, Sacramento,
Washington, and Laguna

The Park closes at midnight.

Brett takes me to Lake Tahoe to camp with friends and their dogs. Here we are at a local South Lake Tahoe restaurant. I don't beg for food but I enjoy sniffing around to see what's on the table.

I basically eat a strictly puppy diet right now because that is best for me. If I get too fat it will be difficult for me to run, chase my friends, and to jump up into the car. Brett feeds me special dog food and vitamins to keep me healthy so I can play all day.

SAN FRANCISCO BEACHES

Once I grew up a little, Brett would take me to Crissy Field Beach in view of the Golden Gate Bridge. I romp on the beach until I tire myself out.

When I shake off the sand, you should see all the people run away from me! Then I chase after them. I think we are playing "Tag, you're it!"

Car parking is tight in San Francisco, but some Taxis and Uber cars will accept dogs if you bring a towel to keep their cars clean.

Crissy Field is in the Marina/Cow Hollow area. Check out crissyfieldcenter.org. There is car parking and bike parking. It is good for kids. It's located in the Presidio of San Francisco.

Crissy Field
1199 E. Beach
San Francisco
Closes at 7:00 p.m.
(415) 561-7752

I don't dig holes very often, but I love digging on Crissy Field Beach. Brett covers over my digging before we leave the beach, so no one will fall into the holes I make.

Alcatraz Island Prison is offshore of Crissy Field. I love the cold sand on my belly. If you are interested in history, there are tours to Alcatraz, a 1.5 mile easy boat trip from Crissy Field Beach.

I don't care about a cultural tour because I'm **a dog**! I would rather dig holes in the sand of Crissy Field and look at Alcatraz Island in the distance. Dogs are not allowed on Alcatraz Island. I am happy on the beach playing fetch and "Tag, you're it."

California Welcome Ctr.
9a.m.–8 p.m. Seven Days a week
Excluding Thanksgiving
and Christmas
Pier 39, Building B, Level 2
(415) 981-1280

For Human's Only:
Alcatraz Tours
(347) 263-8811
departs via Ferry
from Pier 33 near
Fisherman's Wharf in
San Francisco

Brett allows us to stay at Crissy Field Beach playing Fetch until after dark. Friends will come play at the beach too. We call this party at the beach "Yappy Hour."

I drink water and our human friends drink whatever they bring to the beach.

Fetch and catch sticks are my favorite games. I also love my belly rubbed and my ears scratched.

Food, fun, and sticks make me happy. "Please, please, please, throw me one more stick!"

I have made many friends at Crissy Field Beach.

Stinson Beach is a fun place to run around. Brett throws sticks and tennis balls for me to fetch and I'll chase and splash him. I don't surf nor fish, but I do chase my friends, one of my favorite sports. I heard that many years ago The Beach Boys singing group surfed here with their friends.

There are some parking spaces available and a snack bar close to the parking lot. A lifeguard usually is on duty May to mid-September. Don't swim alone because there are Rip Tides and strong currents. I don't swim here but I romp, run, and splash everyone near me. This has been a good day.

To get to Stinson Beach from San Francisco, after crossing the Golden Gate Bridge, take Highway 101 North three miles to Highway 1, Stinson Beach exit 445 B, for CA-1 toward Mill Valley/Stinson Beach, a 35-minute drive from the Golden Gate Bridge on CA Highway 1.

Muir Beach and Mount Tamalpais hiking trails are close by.

Rodeo Beach in Marin Headlands.

In the summer we watch surfers here from up on the cliffside.

Brett brings me here so we can enjoy this special dark pebble sand beach. This is the only beach in California with a certain mineral composition, totally different from all other California beaches. Semi-precious stones wash up on Rodeo Beach but I cannot eat them so I don't care about stones!

I love sniffing the Pacific Ocean breezes and resting on the grass. We don't swim here because there have been shark attacks in the past.

Rodeo Beach is part of the Golden Gate National Recreation Area, in Marin County, 2 miles north of the Golden Gate Bridge, in the Marin Headlands.

SAN FRANCISCO PARKS

Lafayette Park is on a hill in Pacific Heights where I live with Brett.

I run and play in this Park every day so I have many dog friends here. I don't growl or bite anyone so I easily make friends!

Lafayette Park in
Pacific Heights—
the Park is bordered on
Gough, Sacramento,
Washington, and Laguna

Catching the frisbee is so much fun and gives me lots of exercise.

Lafayette Park is a public park and has eleven acres of grass and open spaces for me to run and play. You will meet lots of nice dogs and their owners here.

Visit Lafayette Park and let's have fun! I love it here.

You will recognize me. I'm eighty-five pounds and always smiling!

Many of My furry friends show up in Lafayette Park.

We are a dog pack, similar to a wolf pack but we are much nicer. We eat dog food and not small animals because we dogs are civilized and well-mannered.

Lafayette Park and Alta Plaza Park served as campsites for refugees from the 1906 earthquake and fire.

Alta Plaza Park
Western Edge of Pacific Heights
Bounded by Clay, Jackson, Scott &
   Steiner Streets
Open 5 am–Midnight
(415) 831-5500

Brett and I attend Yappy Hour in Mission Dolores Park. Lots of dogs and their best friends attend. I can watch other dogs run around do tricks, and catch frisbees. There are almost 16 acres of recreation area in Dolores Park. It is fun here!

Dolores Park
Dolores St. and 19th St.
San Francisco

RIV sitting on sofa with his blanket.

Did I tell you I am eighty-five pounds now and growing?
I need an entire sofa all to myself these days!

All dogs who like to prance around in the grass on the waterfront, come to Little Marina Green Picnic Area and make some friends. This is a beautiful park right on the Marina so there will be dogs parading around and people walking to their boats.

Little Marina Green
Picnic Area
3950 Scott Street
San Francisco
(415) 831-5500
Park closes at dark

WINTER IN TAHOE

I love to romp in the snow and chase Brett around.

He snowboards all day and I'll romp around with my friends.

I am so tired after a day of jumping and running in the snow, chasing after my friends.

This sofa feels so good.

I'm going to bed now.

"Goodnight!"

WINTER—AT HOME IN SAN FRANCISCO

We love a lighted Holiday tree on our outside patio. San Francisco can have cold evenings. Brett built us a firepit and I enjoy the warm fire.

Toasted marshmallows on the firepit sound yummy but I am not allowed sweets so I only dream about them, while I wait for Santa to arrive.

When we are not playing outside Brett will dress me up in costumes.

I love the winter holidays but I don't know if I like this outfit. Brett thinks I look cute. I'm not so sure about that. "Why is he laughing?" I feel weird in this coat and hat.

What do you think about my Holiday costume?

I am waiting for Santa to come to our apartment so I can show him my Holiday outfit and tell him what a good boy I have been.

SORRY FOR THE INTERRUPTION!

When I was writing this book about my daily fun activities with Brett in and around San Francisco, we were all suddenly surprised by the COVID-19 pandemic. My human grandma repeatedly called or contacted online every business mentioned here to confirm everyone was still operating as usual.

It's always best to call ahead just to make sure well-behaved dogs are still allowed and the business hours are as stated. Grandma confirmed all facts, and she is always right about everything!

SAN FRANCISCO DAYS

This local coffee shop shares space with a popular Bank.

While Grandma and Grandpa meet with bank officers, Brett walks me around the coffee shop. He makes sure we get our daily exercise wherever we go.

We are both in good shape!

Coffee Cafe & Bank
1560 Van Ness Avenue,
and California
On Nob Hill
(415) 749-0365

Early mornings Brett sometimes takes me to Lafayette Park to run and exercise. Then we go to the Flagship Gym so Brett can workout with a trainer. This is my chance to snooze a little.

I love laying on Brett's clothes and backpack when he's lifting weights and working out. The gym doesn't mind me being here if I'm a good peaceful dog, so I take a nap and be quiet.

I don't think I SNORE or SNORT while sleeping!

Then I notice my good friend Colby has arrived too so I wake up hoping he wants to play. I try and make friends every where I go.

I don't bite anyone or snore so I am well-liked at Flagship Gym. I am a good boy and I am invited inside many stores and restaurants.

Flagship Athletic Performance
(Flagship Gym)
Upper Market Area
160 Church Street
(415) 463-1111
Closes 7:30 p.m.

HIKING AROUND SAN FRANCISCO AND TAHOE

I am always happy to go hiking anywhere with Brett and our friends.

I found these mountain wild flowers on a summer hike in Tahoe near the Squaw Valley Resort property.

Sniffing flowers, grass, dogs, people, and food on a table are some of my favorite activities. I spend a lot of time sniffing because I cannot talk and ask questions.

My nose tells me everything I need to know about my world!

I will follow Brett up any mountain trail.

Here we are hiking Mount Tamalpais. Brett takes me hiking and camping to give me many learning experiences. A group of good friends and their dogs always meet up at the hiking trails. It's a big fun day for all of us. I think Brett likes to tire me out so I'll sleep well at night. He is a good Dad to me.

Dogs are not allowed on most trails at Mount Tam but we are welcome to hike on The Old Stage Road. It's only a .5–.75 mile path and we are allowed to play here. This path leads to the Marin Municipal Water District Land which allows dogs on their 130 miles of trails and unpaved roads on District Lands.

We have to stay leashed and behave properly at all times.

You will need a bath once you get home!

Mount Tamalpais State Park
(Old Stage Road)
801 Panoramic Highway
Mill Valley, CA
(415) 388-2070

TRAVELS WITH GRANDMA AND GRANDPA

Grandma and Grandpa live on the East Coast of the U.S.A. When they visit me in San Francisco we do fun things such as eat in fancy restaurants and ride the ferry to Tiburon where we eat some more, one of my favorite activities.

Training horses and dogs in Florida was one of Grandma's earliest jobs but in San Francisco she practices my tricks with me every day. Did I tell you Grandma travels with Treats just for me?

I will show Grandma my tricks all day long. I love treats! And Grandma is very nice too.

Sometimes I ride in the car with Grandma when we visit Tiburon, across the Bay from downtown San Francisco.

I'm also allowed to ride the ferry to Tiburon if I'm leashed and I'm a good boy. I always behave because I like to go places and have fun with Grandma and family.

Grandma always has tastee treats in her pocket. I remember where treats come from because I can smell treats!

The Blue and Gold Fleet Ferries to Tiburon—leashed dogs are allowed on the ferry to Sausalito and Tiburon. Hours Monday to Friday 9:45 a.m. to 6:45 p.m.

Depart Pier 41 on the Embarcadero. Tours are Fridays, Saturdays and Sundays. The ferry leaves 11:10 a.m. to 6:20 p.m. Check the blueandgoldfleet.com for prices or call them at (415) 705-8200. Thursday to Monday office open at 9 a.m. to 5 p.m.

Brett takes me many places and he makes sure I'm happy and healthy, ready to enjoy life. I'm a lucky dog!

Tiburon loves having us visit. It's a beautiful place to run and walk. There's lots of food and ice cream for me and shopping for Grandma.

San Francisco is directly across the Bay under the white clouds.

I politely ask Grandpa to share his water with me. This is the outside waterfront restaurant area of what used to be Guaymas Mexican restaurant on the Tiburon waterfront.

We take the ferry from San Francisco and dock in front of the restaurant. You can also drive here.

The new restaurant will possibly be opened by a Michelin-starred chef which means the food will be very yummy. I hear the restaurant will be opened soon and hoping the new place will allow me to visit them on their waterfront again.

It's fun to shop, eat, and wander around Tiburon. There are many great restaurants and shops here.

Also stop into Sam's Anchor Cafe at 27 main street. They have good food and a lively dining area on their large deck. Call Sam's and ask if you can dock your boat there. (415) 435-4527. Or you can take the ferry from the Embarcadero to Tiburon. Dogs are allowed on Sam's outside deck.

5 Main St.
Tiburon, CA
Ark Row Shopping Center

NAPA VALLEY DAYS AND NIGHTS

Grandma and Grandpa love bringing me to stay in the Napa River Inn in the Historic Riverfront District in Napa Valley. The Inn welcomes their dog guests with treats, dog bowls, and dog blankets in the rooms. I love TV and they have TV's in every room!

Look how they welcome me here! The INN even writes my name on their dog guest sign out front. It looks like I will have a nice time here.

What a great way to start out my two nights in Napa Valley with Brett and my family.

I can't wait to return here again!

Napa River Inn
in the Historic River Front District
500 Main St.
(877) 251-8500

I snuck into the garden at Napa River Inn to sniff their fragrant flowers. Flowers are prettier than regular grass I sniff in the parks we visit at home.

Napa River Inn welcomes me into their lobby area. This is where the dog treats and refreshments come from so I visit here a lot!

Grandma loves treats and refreshments too so we go together.

When Grandma walks me around historic Napa she loves stopping in the local County library.

Grandma loves to read books. She thinks I understand the stories she reads to me. She thinks I read books too because I am so smart!

Only service dogs are allowed inside the library so I stay outside with friends, waiting for Grandma.

Napa County Library
580 Coombs St.
(707) 253-4241
Monday–Saturday 10 a.m.–5:30 p.m.
Sunday 1 p.m.–4:30 p.m.

Angèle Restaurant on the same block as the Napa River Inn allows well-trained dogs to join their humans on the terrace over-looking the Napa River.

The kind and friendly staff was happy to see me and gave me many tastee treats! I love Napa Valley restaurants!

Grandpa feeds me celery at Angèle. I will eat anything from Grandpa, even green salad!

Brett is my best friend so I am always watching over him and I know he is always looking after me.

I also watch to see what food flies off the table in my direction, so I pay close attention!

I love the food, the setting on the historic river, and especially the friendly staff at Angèle. They bring me treats because I'm a good dog!

Angèle Restaurant and Bar
540 Main St.
Napa Historic District
(707) 252-8115

Napa Valley's Silver Oak Winery allows me to play on their outdoor patio with my human friends. I always listen to Brett's instructions to behave in restaurants and wherever we go because I love traveling with him.

He makes my life fun every day!

Silver Oak Napa Valley
915 Oakville Cross Rd.
Oakville, CA 94562
Closes 5 p.m.
(707) 942-7022

I am well-behaved and am allowed into various Napa wine tasting rooms. Soon I know I'll be walking on the city sidewalks of historic Napa, sniffing the grass and flowers. So I lie down quietly and wait until we go outside where I'll trot along the historic walkways with Brett.

Celadon restaurant gives me the best table in their outside dining area. It's a covered area right in front of the warm fire. I can watch everyone who walks in and out of the restaurant. I think Celadon wanted to show me off so they gave me this special table. Or maybe they wanted me close to the front door just in case I had to run outside all of a sudden?

The short ribs over mashed potatoes here are so good! Grandma loves the Pork Belly and watermelon salad. This is her favorite restaurant on Earth. I think it is my favorite too.

Tucked behind a lighted garden in the Napa Historic Mill.

Celadon
500 Main St., Suite G
Napa, CA
Celadonnapa.com
(707) 254-9690

My cousin Harry travels to Calistoga, California, from the East Coast to walk me through the vineyards. I love to run and play with my family who come to California to visit me. I give them a good work out when they walk me or chase me around.

I bet they sleep well at night too!

DRIVING THE CALIFORNIA COAST SOUTH, ON THE WAY TO OJAI

We drove to Ojai, CA, to visit cousin Mary Ashley, who was having a baby in a few weeks. Here I am again with my best friend Brett. We are a little North of Santa Barbara on a mountain over-looking a beautiful beach. I love taking selfies with Brett and running around the mountainside sniffing the flowers and the Pacific Ocean air.

My nose tells me everything I need to know about my world such as "do chipmonks and squirrels live around here?" I smell something funny. I tried to play with a skunk recently and I now know what a skunk smells like! Pee-yew! Stay away from skunks!

I was put in charge of entertaining sleepy Kernel Biscuit. He belongs to my human cousin Mary Ashley and her husband Keith who live in Ojai.

Guess I tired out Kernel Biscuit unless he's just pretending to be asleep? "Maybe he's ignoring me on purpose?"

I am six years old now and I tire out absolutely everyone!

Soon I leave on a cross-country road trip with my best friend Brett and good friend Bryce. We will drive all the way to New York City and back! I hear Grandpa will ride back to San Francisco with us. That will be a super fun trip because Grandpa is nice and he always feeds me good treats.

I'll be in touch later!

Until our next trip...

The End

About the Author

Charlotte is from Texas. She spent four early years in Istanbul with her military parents. She studied journalism at a Florida University and lived in DC for many years with her husband of thirty-seven years. Their son Brett lives in San Francisco, California, where he and his big Bernedoodle Riv explore the beauty of the San Francisco Bay area.